silk.

D1739028

silk.

silk.

"The highest human act is to inspire."
- Nipsey Hussle

samantha sao

silk.

ISBN: 9798559250823
Email: saosamantha@gmail.com
Instagram: @_lavendersilk_
Website: samanthasao.com

silk.

thank you for inspiring me

samantha sao

healing. happiness is a journey, not a destination.
a constant sail that never stops and is ever-changing
pain. pain is the cargo — the trials and tribulations.
love. love acts as currents of water and wind.
self-love is the ship itself. *you can only find within.*

You. You are the sea. Your waves are pulled by the
moon. Keep your eyes set on shore. Love will get
you there soon. But, we've got some ways to go.

samantha sao

vi

silk.

We are all fighting demons, usually behind closed doors. I want to fight mine in the light — with you. We all face challenges. Sometimes simultaneously, but usually at different speeds. Thank you for being able to connect with me and my journey.

It has been a wild year. There has been loss upon loss. We get broken down, only to be built up again — but with new and thicker skin. Carry your head high, but remember to stay grounded. Take a few moments to yourself. Embrace your worth. Gratitude is important, but remember to treat those negative feelings first.

samantha sao

silk.

The Woman I Am Today

My name is Sopunny Samantha Sao. My parents escaped Cambodia during the Khmer Rouge era, also known as the Killing Fields or Cambodian Genocide. The Khmer Rouge army was led by Prime Minister Pol Pot and his allies. His mission was to create an agrarian society that would eventually lead the country to communism.

Pol Pot's army forced millions of residents from their homes in the city to work on communal farms. He executed or imprisoned anyone that tried to resist, anyone that was educated, anyone who sought religion, and unfortunately, the list continues on. Between 1975 to 1979, approximately 2 million victims were executed by the Khmer Rouge. Millions fled to Thailand for refuge. I wish everyone's story was as successful as my family's.

My parents made it. The walk from Cambodia to Thailand took more than three months. The trek led them through jungles, streams, creeks, and all. It is still very hard for them to talk about. They were torn from their families and witnessed other families be torn apart as well.

I am incredibly grateful. My parents have only shared a fraction of the struggles they've endured. I can't even fathom what sits in their unwanted memories. I am proud to be their daughter and a first-generation American.

They won a chance at a new life in America through a lottery system — yes, it's exactly how it sounds.

Their number was chosen. My mother, who was secretly pregnant at the time, quickly fled the country alongside my father and two sisters. Together, they boarded a plane to Los Angeles, CA.

I was born a decade later on November 17th, as a complete surprise. My sisters were unaware of my mom's pregnancy the entire time. The best surprise, I must say (hehe). We lived on Sunset Blvd. & Elysian Park Ave; a 2 bedroom apartment located right in front of Dodger Stadium.
The heart of LA.

My life has been building up for this moment — this accomplishment. This year has been the year of reflection. I've reminisced about childhood walks to the liquor store, buying raspados in Echo Park, attending family parties with karaoke playing nonstop. I've reminisced about high school, moving to an out of state college, returning home with loans, a mugshot, and what *felt* like a broken heart.

I've reflected on my journey through adulthood; that led me to my current position. I never thought I'd be a poet. I never thought about writing a book, let alone sharing or *publishing* my pieces. That just proves that the only limitations you face are the ones *you create.* We have to stop doubting ourselves, our abilities, and our capabilities. Anything is possible. Just put in the work and believe.

samantha sao

About the Book

silk. is a physical encapsulation of my journey. I have written about the tug of wars between myself, healing, heartbreak, forgiveness, and so much more. I have mountains to climb on this journey of genuine happiness, acceptance, and self-love.
But, I am ready. Will you come with me?

it's hidden under the covers,
immersed in the tears and fear
it's beneath the self-hate
layers of negative self-talk
and other people's opinions

it's here.
find it. embrace it.

create your own fate.

samantha sao

Healing is a journey, not a destination

Take your time
Feel it all

Just remember to treat yourself well when you fall

With gentle hands
Give yourself time to understand
All that your mind demands

You are ever-changing
Its time
Evolve.

samantha sao

The Woman of My Dreams
She's a work in progress
Still a mess
Still the best she can be despite the circumstances
She's beautiful
From LA, so she reps the West
She wants to change the world
One person at a time
What she wants is already hers
It's already mine

I know I needed this for my transformation
There's room for improvement
and I have high expectations
It's Scorpio season and I'm ready
To shed who I was yesterday
and embrace who stands before me

Los Angeles
Home of the Champions
Talk about motivation
The Lakers & The Dodgers —
Just winning & winning
It makes me reminiscent of my childhood
The walks home from school
Through Dodger traffic
Random men on my street
Ticket scalping
All of LA cheers while we watch Kobe play
I even ditched school for the 2010 Lakers parade
More than just memories
Its all imprinted in me
I'm so proud of my city
To live and die in LA

310, 323 & 213!

samantha sao

We grew up with steel bars on our windows
Wearing our siblings' clothes
Were those gunshots or fireworks?
No one really knows

silk.

Both of my earphones drown out the cat calls
It's such a shame that I can't even take a walk
Without men shouting at me from their trucks
Whistles & smooches
I used to flip 'em off
Cuss 'em out & yell back from the sidewalk
Some would drive off and others would be offended
The audacity of me?
I wanna cause a scene
    but, I can't afford to be hot headed

I'm sorry
I think I'm in the wrong place
I've lived here before, but don't see a familiar face
Everyone looks different
Mom & Pop shops taken over by vegan cuisines
Why'd they replace the doctor's office
with a bike shop?
They turned my childhood market
into a fucking gelato spot
No more FASHION FOR EVA
House of Spirits is gone
Damn, they were Cambodian-owned too
I hope they still have a home
Gentrification
What a devastation
What happened to the Echo Park I knew?

silk.

There will come a day when...
I won't have to buy myself flowers anymore
But until then
I'll grab them from the flower mart
or a street vendor

#supportyourstreetvendors

Beauty is in the eye of the beholder
Do you hold me?
Feel the coolness of my hands
and the heat off my cheeks
Put your thoughts on pause
and enjoy the serenity
Surrender to the moment
Now back to reality
in 1, 2, 3

Melanin

I'm sorry I didn't give you the love you deserved
Dark skin was associated with the lower class
The people in the fields, picking rice & cutting grass
I wish I could go back and value it more

I'd apply lightening cream to my 8 year old cheeks
Every day for about 3 weeks
Disappointed every time I looked in the mirror
"Mom, I'm still so dark… how can I look clearer?"

In 5th grade, my sister told me,
"Celebrities *pay* to be your color"
But I didn't believe her
Because everyone around me
Well, they just wanted to be lighter

Now at 23, I can finally be me
No wonder I struggle with self-love & affection
Our ideas of perfection fuel our self-destruction

We are perfectly flawed
And I am teaching myself
How to love them all

samantha sao

Sunlight kisses my skin
Warmth so deeply underrated
I used to despise it
I used to hate it
My melanin made it harder for me to love me
So deep & rich
Now I feel like *I'm that bitch*

silk.

K(no)w
Everyone is so afraid of making the wrong decision
It prevents them from making any
High risk brings high reward
and i'm taking many
Many wins, many losses,
and many tears in between
But comfort should make you uncomfortable
and it makes me want to scream

How many hours have gone to waste?
Occupied by my phone
Staring at my own face
Analyzing my cheekbones
Sucking in my waist

Seeping into the quicksand of Instagram
I have to remember how beautiful
and unique I am

silk.

Seeking validation in today's standard of beauty
Setting myself up for failure each time
The girls we idolize on instagram
don't even claim their own bodies
But here we are
Still trying to keep up with society

What if I never left LA?
Unpacked my bags & decided to stay?
I wonder who I would have turned out to be
Where would I have been in 2020?
The "what-ifs" are irrelevant
They'd probably drive me crazy
I just can't help
but to think of the possibilities

silk.

If I moved out, would I still feel this way?
Stagnate and stuck
But I'm doing ok
I'm only stagnant physically
My mind is everywhere
From the highest heavens to the earth's core
I want to push past the stratosphere
      — and soar, soar, soar!

Release to relieve
Finally, a chance to breathe
>That's why I love the ocean
>So turbulent and intense
>>but, it calms before reaching shore
>>>>>*unlike me*
I am always turbulent
>— inside I am violent
>>I do not know peace
>>>*I can't seem to find it*

silk.

My empathy holds few bounds
I wish smiles conquer your frowns
There's so much love
Inside my soul and yours
Vast oceans of love out there in the world
A cool breeze and gentle waves
I can't lie, sometimes I just wanna set shit ablaze
But right now
I just want to close my eyes
      — *exhale & float away*

Learning to let go of hesitation
Reflect and reminisce
But don't dwell or overthink
Prevent yourself from manifesting negativity
We can be so pessimistic and not even realize it
Focus on the now
Focus on yourself
"What holds my attention? What ignites my spirit?"

silk.

To my soulmate
I want to feel safe with you
like if I'm stuck at sea ~
You would change the currents to come find me
When my head is stuck in the clouds
or my energy is low
You sit beside me
and allow me to rest on your soul

samantha sao

*You were the fire
I was the air*

*It was a disaster
I wasn't prepared*

silk.

If I could go back to those times at the beach
I would.
                in an instant
                    in a *heartbeat*
The stars were out
I saw them in your eyes
I'm still so confused
I guess my intuition didn't see the flags
The ash of our fire coated them
Disguised them as white
But I was the one who surrendered
To my surprise

One in a Million

Infinite stars in the sky
But your shine was the one that caught my eye
You are my reality
This feeling is more than a high

I could write you a 4 page letter
And seal it with a kiss
So you can go back and read it
Whenever you'd like to reminisce

Inspired by Aaliyah, RIP

silk.

I see my reflection
I wonder who she is
    What she loves
    What she fears
They're all coming alive
The trials are in session
What am I to do?
Resort to my old self?
Or empower the new?
Tell me who can I run to
On days like this
I've been up since 2 am
Tryna Xscape,
    But instead I reminisce

Thank you, Hip-Hop
Where would I be without you?
I was rapping along to Biggie & 'Pac
Unaware it was you I was listening to
In middle school, I heard my first
A Tribe Called Quest song
Find A Way changed my life
Lyrical geniuses
Q-tip, Jarobi, Ali & Phife
I found my way to Snoop & Dre
I still rap every word to Cube's
"Today Was a Good Day"
In high school, I hated mumble rap
I wanted the lyricists back
I wanted meaningful messages, not broads
shaking they ass & crevasses
The more I grew up,
I learned to appreciate it all
Thank you, Hip Hop
You been beside me
Entangled in my earphones
Uplifting me through each fall

silk.

If i were to skydive, would you be my parachute?
slow me down from crashing
I may tumble or trip
but i'll be okay
you're worth it

a safe landing

What happens to the things we never say?
We think it goes away
but really, it builds & piles
Until you can't take it anymore
& you talk for miles
— run, run, run
On the path of emotions & reaction
It's like nothing ever happened
The whole situation was one-sided
and you didn't feel a fraction

silk.

Maybe i'm the fool
Giving you the push and letting you pull
me into another failed situationship
I let your hands trace my hips
as i kissed your fingertips
I felt so warm and safe
but you didn't know what to do
what to say, how to say it, or when
— you don't have to say anything anymore
Instead of feeling the comfort of your warmth
I feel the chill of the wind

We have a connection
But we're on different spectrums
You love to lust me
& I lust to love you

There was a point where I thought you felt the same
way too
       I was wrong — again
       I mistook your openness for vulnerability

Don't worry,
I've learned my lesson

silk.

I don't know if i'm a lover or a fighter
'Cause when I reach out, I get caught up
Searching for love is my first mistake
Unrealistic expectations stem
from the love we see on TV
The kind we watched on Disney
Rose petals and kisses on my doorstep
I don't think i've had either yet

In my own lane
At my own time
You can find me
I'm not hard to find
But until then, i'll see you around
While i'm scrolling through my timeline
or looking at a cloud
This isn't new, but it's necessary
I'm sorry I don't believe you
when you say you want me
I've just heard it all before
Can you blame me?
Actions speak louder than words
  and there's no sound to me

silk.

The way the light shines
Leaves me blind
I reach out for warmth,
only to get burned every time

You can't hurt me
if i don't let you close

but how else
would i feel
your warmth?

I know what I'm looking for
I won't find
but these temporary situations
kind of
ease my mind

silk.

I treat your energy as a French inhale

There's a million things about you
I still have to discover
Guide me through
I can help you uncover
Your favorite memories
and the ones that are hard to remember
Just hold my hand
Let's walk through them together

Another Bruised Ego

I thought you were falling for me too
Why am I the only one that's black & blue?

It's like you set me up to jump into this
But when it was time to let go
Your feet never left the pavement

I enjoyed the fall
Unaware that you weren't there
I looked up
I couldn't find you
I still can't find you anywhere

This isn't new
I thought "Damn, I've never met anyone like you"
I tried to be optimistic
and look at it from a positive point of view
This is why I talk to fuck boys
At least I know their intentions

Now my heart tightens whenever I hear that
question

silk.

"What's up? What happened with you & him?"
The same as the others
He left

Now I have to pick up the pieces
I should consider it theft

You were an undercover crook
I let you in
So foolish
A fool once again

I laid with you
Showed you a side only my best friend knew
I never even read her my poems...
before I read them to you

We were supposed to fall together
Why am I the only one that's black & blue?

I hope Julie & i fall in love at the same time
But if it were to be me or her, i hope she finds it first
I hope she gets picnics in the park
and reassurance from the heart
I can wait
I've waited this long
I'll catch the bouquet at her wedding
while we dance to a Bad Bunny song

Kind souls are meant to console

\

To the Moon
Thank you for all you do
I might like you more than the Sun
But that's a secret between me & you
                          secrets from the sun

silk.

There's something about the night that makes me
want to stay up
Put my dreams on hold & just lay up
There's a sweet peace to it…

The darkness & the sound
Even on the wildest nights with good friends around

I can't wait for social distancing to end
So i can hug them all again

Zoom parties & texts can only do so much
I'm a human in need of human touch

samantha sao

Reaching out for someone to hold my hand
To understand
All of the things my mind demands
And to tell me *it's okay*
      I don't have to abide
      I don't have to obey
Life doesn't happen one way
I can go whichever direction i desire
All these options
      I just want the one that's right
      But if it were that easy,
            we wouldn't reach any heights

silk.

Smoke & broken mirrors
Yearning for a place to think clearer
A million things on my mind
Where to begin? How to unwind?
Focus, focus, focus
I have a group presentation
Crap, when's my next test?
I'm hanging on
but i'm slipping
— reaching for the next check
Is this what adulting is? Is it all worth it?
I need something fulfilling
I need to find my purpose

"I am in control of my emotion"
I tell myself at least

My feelings are as turbulent as the sea
Sometimes calm, Sometimes violent

I wish I could show you what I see.
Then you'd realize why i'm so bent
— *out of shape and proportion.*

You were supposed to be my protector,
my confidant, and my best friend
but it's fine

I love you so much, i'll carry the blame
— *for now at least*
but to be perfectly honest

I don't know how long
I can let this fuck up my peace

silk.

Lay up
Maybe this is the assist i need
The virus picked up speed…
Took off and never looked back
From country to country, it was a guerilla attack
Traveling penalties and double dribbles
This shit is foul and the injury is critical
I never thought i'd be in this position
It's like i tore my achilles
and the rookie got subbed in
So many tears and good-byes for hundreds of
terminations
What's the plan?
It feels like y'all cut us with no hesitation
I know that's not right
It's happening all over
630k claims for unemployment
Will it end by November?
I'll just focus on school and keep to myself
Finally, i have time to prioritize
my physical and mental health

March 17th, 2020

This much time alone scares me
Too many things to face
Thoughts i've shoved to the back of my brain
Filed away in color-coded sections of pain

Childhood trauma
Even as an adolescence
Toxic adult patterns
Help me learn my lessons

Let me change the currents
I can swim upstream like the salmon do
Escape the birds, the bears
And the other animals that need food too

Help me leave this time of isolation
with a better understanding of me
What do i like
Who do i love
And who the F i wanna be

quarantine

'Rona & Riots
Who knew that'd be 2020?
How will I raise my son when he's ready?
He'll have rich, brown skin
How do I teach him to love it
when society will punish him for it?
Every look
Every drive
Every traffic stop
He'll have generational trauma
whenever he sees a cop
"Mama always told me to be proud of my melanin
— but even if I comply, I could be a victim"

Rioting & looting
The system is abusing
Innocent civilians & taking their lives
                    "I can't breathe, Mama help me"

Another viral video, another body bag
So many names to acknowledge, what a painful
time

Hate crimes on Asians
Aussie girls pullin' knives
Latinx babies caged up in detention centers
with tears in their eyes
The virus is roaring,
but that's not the real pandemic

Racism is an illness
Point blank period.

silk.

We were raised to believe Black wasn't beautiful
Brown isn't either

A high school boyfriend gave me tips
on how to remove the pigment from my body
Scrub, scrub, scrub
Because, "Asians weren't supposed to look dirty"
Ignorance
Ignorance bred by previous generations of the same

I wish i could talk to my younger self
And tell her to embrace everything she tried to hide
But i can only talk to myself now
And unlearn everything i was taught somehow

My cousin got out of jail today
This should be a time for celebration
Unfortunately
He'll be taken into ICE custody
Sent back to where he came
Locked up 20 years
20 years of being called
a number instead of a name
Do I have a right to be sad? We never even met
It just breaks my heart
That's a moment we won't be able to get
A tragedy
The system doesn't give a fuck about humanity
Adults in cages
Children in cages
I'm sure they've lost their sanity

silk.

Good news
His lawyer & supporters were able to deter him
from ICE custody
Today was so beautiful
Even though, we could only connect virtually
We could feel all of the emotions
From family, friends, peers
Such love & gratitude in the air
I am so happy he's no longer in solitude
Thank you for all of your prayers
I am so blessed to live the life I do
With beautiful souls all around me
To be able to wake up
and drive wherever I desire to be
Oh, the things we take for granted
                    — *freedom, independence, & sanity*

My heart is so heavy
But it doesn't outweigh my mind
A million thoughts running on overtime
I usually worry about the past
      or what's gonna happen next
           but right now,
               I'm worried about the present
                  & its fucked up tricks
In the end, the very end
There's a bigger picture
      But God, please help me see it clearer

silk.

I've been waking up with tears in my eyes
I don't want to get out of bed
How is it fair for me to rise
and you can't?

You deserved more
So much more
We hold onto your memories
Pray for you on bended knees

I can still
Feel your energy
Hear your laugh
Hear your sass

I wish i would have known
that the last time i saw you
would truly be the last

It all happened too soon
It happened too fast

This is the first morning
I wake up without tears flowing down my cheeks
My tear ducts often break free
and create salt water creeks
I can't cry anymore
I don't want my tears to keep you here
What's next in the after life?
Where does your spirit roam at night?
Ascend
Heaven receives you
Your vision has been restored
You now have wings
Baby girl, you must soar
I pray your soul finds peace
& joy eventually
All i can say is
Thank you for all that you have done for me

RIP E.D. ♡

a beloved mother, daughter, sister, and friend

silk.

It'll be okay
Even if it's not
You get to move on and we can figure it out
Nothing lasts forever
— that's apart of life's beauty
I hope i'm all you expected of me
A Grandfather to 40 grandkids & more
Please tell Grandma i said hi when you make it
to heaven's door

Now Auntie's gone & i hope she finds you
I pray she finds peace,
a feeling she never knew

RIP Tha & RIP Ming

I am so blessed to be able to get an education
That opportunity was not attainable for my parents
Definitely not in Cambodia
Higher learning was forbidden
If you were educated, you were considered a threat
And ordered to be killed
Whether you were a doctor
or just owned a pair of glasses
They assumed you could read
            — and couldn't take their chances
You were a danger
to the dictator's picture perfect society

My parents escaped death numerous times
and even helped others along the way
But to those they couldn't help, we still light an
incense for them 'til this day

When they came to the states
All they knew was survival
No English, no drivers license,
and definitely no iPhone

silk.

They had to learn a trade and stick to it
So they decided to sew
Sweatshop conditions
— the wages are so, so, so low

But they made it work
It makes me think about my own complaints
Damn I feel like a jerk

I know my dad wishes he knew more English
He is such a smart man
So gentle and forgiving

I asked him what he wanted to be as a little boy
What kind of careers was he exposed to in the
1960's?

He couldn't give me an answer
"I just wanted to live..." he told me

I need more than a check to check lifestyle
Ma, I hope you see it
It's coming, I promise
I will repay you
For all of the heartbreak
And all of the hardships

Mom's getting older
I feel the weight on my shoulders
Luckily I have my sisters as soldiers
We're tryna break generational curses
The trauma exceeds boulders
But I was born ready
I am a warrior

silk.

I have a lot of healing to do
But that journey will last a lifetime
There's beauty in the process
I know, I know, I know
I wanna embrace the beauty in me
How much longer do I have to go?

You deserve it
What if i told you...
Most of the thoughts you think of yourself
are untrue
You are deserving
You are clever
You are kind
Your energy is felt through space
You create your own time

Why is it so hard to remain kind?
Why does self-deprecation come effortlessly?
But when it's time to applaud yourself...
you suddenly freeze

I hope you can learn how to feel at ease
In your own thoughts
You can't escape yourself
And when you *think* you do...
It only goes far

silk.

Escapism is real
Escapism doesn't help you heal
Instead it delays and reroutes
You could have gotten there earlier
but you were buried in doubts

I challenge you
to love yourself harder
On the days you don't wanna bother
The days when you want to
fold like fresh laundry
& stay tucked under the sheets

I challenge you to free yourself from the quicksand
of your thoughts & defeat
Don't get me wrong, we all deserve breaks
But you also deserve to enjoy and
love yourself
with every breath you take

To the woman I was last year
Why live in fear?
Instead of thinking...
>*what's the worst that can happen?*
You have to think...
>*what's the best possible outcome?*
Manifest it
Put in the work & leave the rest to God
Fate
The universe
Whomever sits at the top of your soul
Yes, to live with less fear
That's my goal

silk.

Her glow is illuminating through her seams
Her eyes are made of honey
So are her thighs
A heart made of gold
What made her so cold?
The strongest thing to do
is to remain soft in this world

Love is pure
Love absorbs parts of me that are insecure
When life turns my fears into reality,
Love comes in & carries me through
Self-love hits differently
When you realize its much deeper
Than just feeling pretty

silk.

Don't get too close
The warmth will seep in your skin
Through your muscles
and into your bones
You'll think he's the one
and it's not the same to be alone
Tunnel vision
Your phone becomes your focus
Its glued to your hand
like the stem of a lotus
Heart eyes & lol's
All that hocus pocus
but what am i to do?
Codependency is my enemy
& I want to be okay without you

We're losing our spark
I just want a day at the park
where we lay on a blanket
and watch the clouds
So cliché, but i'm just thinking out loud
You think i wanna be taken to boujie restaurants
for shrimps and steaks
I guess that's what i get for not setting the standard
of our dates
Maybe you're apart of the cycle
and nothing's gonna change
You'll be a memory in a few months
and i'm back to the same
Swipe right, swipe left, swipe away my mistakes
Maybe i'm just in my head
and we'll be okay

silk.

I should have known
This always happens
The feeling is rarely mutual
What about me is so undesirable?
I've been thinking
Maybe I'm not ready to receive
I gotta let shit go
My hands are callused from holding onto the past
Maybe I'm not ready to give...
Why do I always fall so fast
I feel my heart tighten
I visualize you in my head so often
Tell me what you want
Or what you don't want
Tell me you want me...
But if that's not it
Then please leave
How foolish of me
To allow you to disturb my peace

In my feelings today, but what's new
I say that like I didn't feel this way yesterday
I guess my favorite color is blue
      I'm ashamed of feeling so pressed
       knowing your hands are on her breasts
It's none of my concern
Do you
She can have my parking spot
But you best log out of my Hulu

silk.

Damn you're hard to read
But I'm caught up on you
lost at sea
Your thoughts are written in braille
I wanna get to know you well
Tell me your fears
What gives you goosebumps?
Tell me the good, the bad
dimé
tell me the pointless stuff
You don't have to worry when you're with me
All your secrets are safe
That's what I can be for you
A safe space

I'll lay out a blanket
Pillows & all *that*
I open my heart to you
It even has a welcome mat

Success

What is its true definition?
Is it tangible or can you feel it?
Would it be…
Living anxiety-free, giving birth to a healthy baby,
or is it a realtor handing over a new set of keys?
All of the above?
Without one, you can't have the other
The desire to be a mother, lover, or a brother
The desire to give back to the community
& change lives
It all starts right here,
like looking into a stranger's eyes
Make sure they know their presence is loved
and cherished
and without them,
someone's world would perish

Pay a compliment
or even a simple "thank you"
Lead with kindness
You never know what others are going through

silk.

He asked me, "Do you know who you are?"
I said, "I don't know, I'm not really sure"
I swear i'm trying to figure it out
Is this the right way to go?
Maybe that wasn't the answer you wanted
I can't help, but speak my truth
The pieces will fall
and land where they're meant to
I'm tryna get the same feeling
Kobe had with basketball
Ali & the gloves
Tyson & the doves
I know its coming
I just have to find that love

In a weird state of mind
Everything is *fine*
I can handle it all
I was pushed & now i'm on a free fall
All gravity, no parachute in sight
But, something feels incomplete
  like the moon without night

Numb
That's the point i've reached
You trip me over my own feet
Every time your lips meet
Slurs and nonsense
You say you don't care about us
and you'd rather have a son
Well damn
We tell each other you don't mean it,
but we all know you do
I bet your son wouldn't hug or kiss you like your
daughters do
Maybe it's bigger than me
Alcoholism is a disease
and perhaps you want to be free
You can't escape, you don't even see the issue
This time when you cried
— I walked away
I couldn't even look at you

I am the sky
My mind gets cloudy and my heart feels polluted
Tears roll down my cheeks & fall to the trees

I exhale a sigh of relief
It's finally stopped
The sky clears & sunbeams peek through

That is how i hope to feel soon

silk.

Sooner Than Later x Drake

The lights don't glow the same way that they used to
I dropped my rose colored lenses
Picked 'em up to see scratches & cracks
That's what happened with us
It turns out you didn't have my back
Your glow was golden, your aura so angelic
I could have sworn you were heaven sent
Time passes
Your glow is dim now
I see how you move now
Maybe this isn't what I thought
Maybe I was too persistent
Too aggressive
Too willing to get undressed quick
Your goodbye message said everything but that
You said, "I appreciate you. Thank you for adding
value to my time back"
Do you see why I feel the way I do?
If you were in this position, you'd be confused too
Told me one thing,
but your actions proved otherwise
That's why I don't sugar coat
They just prove to be lies

"I love you"
I always thought those words were so special
Instead, it's used for manipulation
To persuade me to stay in a shitty situation
You chose the wrong woman
'Cause I'm **never** settlin'

silk.

I woke up sad
Still can't believe you left shit like that

I'm bitter. I'm angry. I'm mad.

You forced yourself in
Scaled my walls
Maneuvered through the barbed wires
Made me list my flaws & all

Damn, you deserve an award
A round of applause

Was it all an act?
I thought it was real

I'm sorry for talking shit
        I'm just hurt

Out of all the men to leave me bruised
You're one of the worst

I am not special to you
But I am special to me
And that in itself
should push me to leave

silk.

False lashes and crease cuts
It's like all these guys look for are big butts
To each their own
But if that's what you're looking for,
don't hit my phone
You'll say you like me,
I'll tell you its mutual,
But i end up alone
Maybe that's where i need to be
To be forced to let go
And love myself independently

Last line given by @lostmuse_

samantha sao

There are so many men out there
But right now, all I see is you
Every buzz I feel
I wish it was you

I don't want to feel
I don't want someone new
I just want to move on
& pretend I never met you

It wasn't that serious
You really got me delirious
I want to fight my tears...
    but do I really have to?

I should walk away from someone
who doesn't feel the same
    but i'm addicted to the blame & feeling
    ashamed

I guess I don't want good for myself
I guess I don't value my mental,
spiritual,
or physical health

silk.

You got me going through it
and we didn't even do much…
All it took was your touch
Your honey gaze made me feel like it was just us
As if we were the last people in the world

It didn't mean shit
'Cause you don't want me as your girl
You value my sex more than you value my existence
But don't get me wrong, I do feel free
No longer like a rented CD
Baby i'm *vinyl*
          like a record from the '80s
Too bad I grew up in a world
that taught me to hate me

Maybe i was
Chasing after love
Lesson upon lesson
Similar experiences leaving me with the same
question
I'm so disappointed
I feel disposable
I really thought i meant more to you
      I can do better
      I know i will
            You just made it feel so real
Easily finessed
By a guy i didn't even like that much
How can I be strong
when I receive the right touch?

silk.

You leave in 4 weeks
Maybe I was right
This was a summer fling
You'll be filed in my past, "Summer of 2020 "

Damn, we really fell in lust during quarantine

Malibu isn't the same without you
Our bodies are still imprinted in the sand
Our first kiss in the waves, by the caves
Fuck
Missing you comes in waves

It's crazy to know
That spending time with me
Isn't on your itinerary
The next time
You come to our city

/

silk.

I couldn't help but to think of you
I see cars pulled over to the side
Remember when that was you & I?

You made sure we were under the moon and stars
You knew that was important to me

Shit like that makes it hard to believe
That you were only here to deceive
Me,
My intuition,
My mind

I should have known
Our moment together was timed

Our souls met
I'd call that a cosmic collision
Why us
Why not?
Who makes that decision?

Some connections are meant to fall apart
Millions of people walk around with broken hearts
A head full of thoughts
— a phone full of 'em too
Talking to 10 different women

Just desperately
trying to forget
You.

silk.

I'm slipping
Past the shoreline
into the waters
Thinking about us after hours
You felt like ecstasy
So good
unreal
I will always chase
The high you made me feel

I can be emotional & strong, right?
I can cry while I fight & still hold my ground
…*right?*
Is that a juxtaposition?
I can't talk to anyone
Not even those that'll listen
Most of my troubles are internal
Fuck, I need a therapist — *a licensed professional*

silk.

These men can smell it on you
Weakness, fragility
The desire to be secure in vulnerability
You wear your petals like armor
And your leaves like shields
But he plucks them anyway
Petal by petal
Clasp by clasp
& when he's done with your beauty
He tosses you in the grass
i am a field of flower stems

You played with my emotions
And kept me hoping
That one day you'd be my man
And finally, i'd be able to open
And tell you all of the secrets
I've been meaning to share
But... i hit you up when i arrived
& you weren't there
I blew your phone up
and you probably silenced it
Damn
4 fucking years i was blinded
Caught up on the idea of your potential
The way you let me down was never gentle

silk.

So why am I surprised now?
It took you so long to tell me the truth

"I was working shit out with my baby mama,
but now it's you... I'm thankful you're available
whenever I come around… I thought a good man
would've snatched you up by now"

And the stupidest part is that i listen
Like the fool i've always been
But fuck that
I'm over it, i'm over you
And all of these thoughts you had me misconstrue
Don't hit me in 2020
I promise I'll be somebody new

Drugs are not the answer
People use substances as a remedy
When they're really a cancer
There are different ways to cure your pain
— other ways to relieve your brain
We weren't close, but I am so sad
I don't even have to close my eyes…
I can still see your smile & hear your laugh
Drugs are the devil in disguise
I hope your spirit can return home
Rest In Peace Friend,
I am so grateful to have known

silk.

The pain is aching again
Secrets feel like boulders
But i'll carry the weight

I'd rather endure it
than have you feel the pain
Things are picture perfect from the surface
You're blessed thats all you get to see

The trigger is still so close to me
Its the reason i've been so cold to me
Its the reason for my hypersexuality

"Its aching again
But it'll stop someday."
I promise myself
It'll be fine
I'll be okay

samantha sao

I've been giving away pieces of myself
ever since I could remember
No wonder i'm dismembered
whenever i look in the mirror.

silk.

I wanna tell you I miss you
But will that scare you away
Or will you surprise me
and decide to stay?

samantha sao

I let you consume me totally
From my head to my toes
I relinquish control

My walls descend
You wrap bandages around my wounds
Neosporin & all

We don't always get it right
But isn't that a part of the fall?

The excitement and the thrill
Look in my eyes
Tell me how you feel

silk.

I miss your memes & your lips
But it's not enough
I allowed myself to be vulnerable
I surrendered my self to your touch
Expressed my emotions & you declined
My ego is so bruised
I've been so used,
but I'd rather be here
Being used by you
     Suck me dry
     Until i'm depleted
You touch my skin as if it were velvet
You know my body better than a ventriloquist
knows his puppet
Goosebumps on my skin like a cool breeze
You're so handsome, you open me up with ease
Bad decisions can only last so long
Nothing is permanent
But tell me
     Is this really where we belong?

Thank you
for caring about me
And my poems too
You try to fulfill my needs
Even before I do
You're so handsome
Your soul is rich
You don't even say the word "bitch"
I like to hear you say other things
like my name and your moans
Are you sure you're not made of gold?
You leave flakes of sweat on me when we're done
This is more than just having fun
I feel the connection more than your erection
I feel trust more than lust
You build me up & fill me up
You're my 4 leaf clover, my many strokes of luck

silk.

Our chemistry spoke louder than my will to leave
Even when i do
I end up at your door
I float back to your shore like seaweed
I'm entangled in your eyes
You release between my thighs
Next thing you know i'm out the door
I can't help but to wonder
What you're really here for...

Newness is all I know
Skim the surface, but don't poke past it
Temporary satisfactions over the ones everlastin'
The deeper the wound, the longer it takes to heal
I need an adrenaline rush
I need somethin' to feel.
Jump on, it's all fun & games
Then your heart drops to the pit of your stomach
& you get hit with the pain
But you continue to go on more rides & adventures
Now this one is *fast*
It flies at a hundred miles per hour
I'm having fun
Let me go again
I don't give a fuck about the pain
Let me feel it again

silk.

To the friends that didn't say goodbye
Its okay
And maybe that's what bothers you
The colors that bled from me — deep & through
Pale pinks, violet blues
They ruined the canvas you painted me on
Ignored me, like the alarm on your phone
I'll let you sleep
Hit snooze all you need
I hope there comes an end to all of your crying
For now i'll let you be
So you can
experience these moments without me

samantha sao

Soft strumming
Sweet humming
This beat feels so warm to me
like 80 degrees under green palm leaves

I want you to feel like this when you read my poetry
I want the voice in your head to say,

"Woah, I went through something similar..
This moment she's describing...
Well, its so familiar.."

Allow the warmth of my voice to calm your mind
My words dance and disperse
to create their own time
Interpret each line for yourself
There's no right or wrong answer
Feel it however you'd like
What you see as rose petals
I may see as spikes

silk.

I don't wanna distance myself from you
I want the opposite
I wanna lay with you in my apartment
Let's stay up and discuss our accomplishments
It's a shame you don't feel the same
I can't lie, i been feeling hella blue
You were a fling
I can't stop thinking
Unfortunately
I remember everything about you

samantha sao

Many men try to pursue
Interactions with me, but what's new?
Low — *like the bed pinned to your floor*
No box springs or a bed frame
Just a sock on your door
I'm tired of these flings that last 4 weeks
I tell you i like you
On my champion shit like i'm Meek
A week passes by and i feel the distance
I know when i'm not wanted anymore
And shit changes in an instance
You string me along
So I'm there for your convenience
& I endure it
Because you're my weakness

silk.

Nah, you got me fucked up
I'm nobody's plan b and i wish you luck...
To find another like me?
It'll be tough
I know you can find someone else
Someone better for you
But i know
I can find that shit too
It's so hard being single out here
Everyone likes to play games and nibble on your ear
Open your car door and kiss on your feet
But at the end of the day, can you listen to me?
Do you care about the highs and the lows i'm
feeling?
I cared about yours even through my own healing
You should have gotten your shit together
Before i caught feelings
But now its whatever, because *that feeling is fleeing*

samantha sao

I understand if you don't want to
But I need you to come thru
I wanna escape the chaos
And find paradise in your arms

silk.

Self medication
I used to pick up the phone
and hit you with no hesitation
No reservation
I can't do that anymore
It's not my place
I miss you
and your gold chain
dangling in my face

I'm overreacting again
I know i am
Why am i thinking of the end when we barely
began
I've just been down this road before
Things are soft in the beginning,
but end up hurting me to my core

Is it me and my aggression? My built up sexual
tension? I need to release
But the discipline in me does not defeat the beast
I am my own worst enemy
There's a war zone in my head
A thousand casualties and counting
Before i go to bed
Fantasies upon fantasies, what is my reality?

The solution is to change my perception
I'm searching for the answer
to all these complex questions

silk.

You touched my soul with those brown eyes

Ghosted

My eyes water, but the tears don't fall
Unlike me
I fell
Bruised knees
Bruised ego
You said you didn't want to be one of those men
But look at you
You didn't even call it quits
Didn't you think of my feelings
Not even a little bit?

silk.

I'm tired of mourning people that are alive
I thought I was okay

Now I'm sitting on the bathroom floor
Tryna figure it out
What were the signs?
Was it something I said?
Am I really that blind?

How could I trust you so fast?
You even recited my poems & pumped my gas
It made me melt
I hate dating as a millennial
These boys are from hell

You describe me as the one that got away
But none of your actions made me want to stay
Constant yelling and stern tones
You were in a rough spot and felt alone

I tried to help, but you wanted too much
From a 19 year old who took the fucking bus

You wanted dinner to be made
So I'd get out of work
uber to Ralph's, buy the groceries,
and uber to your place

Chopping away in your kitchen
I'd try to tell you a story
But you didn't want to listen

I'd uber back home around 3 am
So stupid of me to do it over and over again

When I told you I was drained
You mocked me and said,
"You act like I hit you…"
But what you didn't acknowledge
Was that my mind was bloody blue

silk.

"Who you with? You f'n another dude? Who dropped you off? I ain't trippin, you the one with a attitude."

It was the worst 6 months
He still hits me up

He apologizes,
"Sam, you wouldn't understand.
Shit was going down hill.
I was losing my manhood.
You'll never understand how that feels."

I stayed
For as long as I could
I didn't wanna abandon him
I knew everyone else would.

But your peace of mind
is no longer my responsibility
When the person that's supposed to show me love
Is the reason for my injuries.

He took me to hometown buffet as a "test"
Lord, I should have known
I should have known this was gonna be a mess
I should have known you weren't gonna last

After hometown buffet we had another date

I pulled up to a gas station & said,
"Woah woah, wait"
Called him up & said,
"Yo… am I in the wrong place?"
He said,
"Nah that's it! The food is bomb, I swear by it."

I'm in no way a gold digger
But I am a woman of taste
I can pay for my own shit
I really don't hesitate

silk.

Was it too much to expect?
I carry this shame because I still stayed
He wasn't all bad
If he read this, I'm sure he'd be sad
But I really wonder where his head was

I wore heels & a leather jacket
To sit by a checkout line & tear hot sauce packets

I'm in no way a gold digger
But I am a woman of taste
That shit woulda been fine
If you told me that was the plan

I would've shown up prepared
My expectations low
Just like my standards
Just like my boundaries

I knew I should have curved you
I should have stayed lonely

Who summoned these ghosts from my past?
I can't even say I miss you
Because I don't want you back

How could I miss someone
who didn't help me stay afloat?
How could I miss you
when you treated me like a joke?

I can't believe I even kissed him
What does he expect me to say to his DM?

"I hope all is well, you lookin' good as hell..
I'm sorry about how shit ended, I'm missin' you
still..."

I can't reciprocate the same energy
The situation is dead to me

Why do you think you can come back?
What makes it so easy?

silk.

I like you
But I don't trust you
Sadly, that's what i've learned from these situations
Monday would be cool,
but Wednesday you could be gone
Another project or a video for a song
I don't look like those girls & i get insecure
I find satisfaction knowing my heart is pure
But it isn't enough to stop me from overthinking
You say you like me too,
but i've been down this path
Forgive me for being negative
& thinking this connection will pass

Maybe i'm not as healed as I thought
I'm already thinking of where to go if we don't work
out
Who's next? Who's waiting for my text?
Easy fix — *rebound sex*
Who's gonna fill me up now that you're gone?
Who's gonna fill the void you left?
The physical replacement is easy, the emotional will
take too long
So ima hit up Ty because he knows what to do
He's not as toxic as Him, Jim or any of those other
dudes...
I can't follow through with this
It's just you I miss

I can't leave you alone
But should I?
How many times do I need to hear
"Yes, I want you here"
Words of Affirmation
Cease my hesitation
I love the reassurance
I show you appreciation through Acts of Service
Quality Time & Physical Touch go hand in hand
Like the stars & the sky
Like the waves & the sand

these are all gifts

I've been questioning myself
My kindness, strength, knowledge
    Why is it so easy to be negative?
        — but so hard to remain positive?

silk.

I just feel sad
I want to cry and unleash this tension
I tried to confide in you
but you ended up rambling
On and on about yourself
It's not malicious, but didn't you think to mention
Or to ask?
You didn't have a single question
I guess its my mistake
I should just continue to vent to myself

I can't blame you for not feeling the same way
I led myself on by thinking I could control my
emotions
I thought i'd monitor my heartbeat
and remind myself you don't feel the same

But last night, I thought you did
I didn't tell you everything
But I told you enough to scare you off

At least I laid it out and I give myself just one day to
sit and pout
My eyes still water
Knowing i'm not going to see you
Or laugh with you
Or lay
But life goes on
& maybe next time
I won't give my power away

silk.

I've never orgasmed
I've never been in love

why do i settle for less than i deserve

samantha sao

You are my drug
Your eyes are my weakness
You pop up on my phone
and I'm on the 5 freeway in an instant

You are not my home
You are my Motel 6
An escape for the night
I head home after a few hits
Now I know
What they mean
when they call it
dope d*ck

silk.

Why
Why do you do this to yourself?
Running back to a man
so detrimental to your health
You've come so far to throw it all away
So why do you think about him every day?
Is it because there's no one current
to make you feel?
You would rather clutter your time
with toxicity than to heal
"This time'll be different...
he'll let me know if he can't make it"
Wrong
        But what'd you expect?
        We've been through this already
You don't value my time
You drain my energy
        How am i 20-something & still so empty?

How many nights have I cried over you?
While you were laying with someone new
It's none of my business, but I wanna know
Maybe it'll stop the pain & let me grow…
From you
This experience
I have to realize it wasn't true intimacy
It was easy access

silk.

People always ask me why i'm so angry
But i disguise my sad eyes with furrowed brows
And a resting bitch face
Don't come too close
Don't invade my space
I can't afford it
I'm tired of the chase
Leave me alone
I'm tired of the mistakes

My insecurity still eats at me,
but I've been feeling great
Shoutout to the men that inspired my poems
& helped me create
No need to hit me up though
It's too little too late

silk.

Is quarantine fucking y'all up that bad?
For you to come back and cry about what we could
have had?
It sucks to fuck up
But the door is closed
Double bolted & sealed
Thank you
The change of direction allowed me to heal

It sucks
To like someone more than they like you
You tell them, "I miss you"
                    but they never say, "I miss you too"
Ouch
It feels like rejection
Your name gets brought up during casual
conversation
Damn
The connection isn't mutual
It hurts
Why don't you feel the same way
I'm willing to do so much
Beyond the touch
I'd catch several flights for you a month
            But only if i'm invited
                    Here I go again, getting too excited
This is why I don't talk to "good guys"
My mind can't take the violence

silk.

My poison is my remedy
Sometimes I think its on my side
But it turns out to be my enemy

Messy healing
Healing hurts
I'd consider 'em growing pains

This is the time to master growth
You have to break your cycles
Do things differently if you're sick of the same

It won't be linear
It won't be easy

You might not be able to heal **completely**

But I promise
You will feel
Way more free
Way more happy

silk.

I wish I could say i'm tired of writing about you
But I can't lie to myself
It triggers the artist in me
     All of the emotions
     These falsified notions
Thank you Disney
For finding Prince Charming for the woman
I could never be
Self-assured & financially stable at 18

"I don't send men paragraphs anymore"
I used to overshare my feelings
But what for?
I've been on the receiving end
I've picked up the phone
And ignored the notification
I refuse to put myself in that position
A man that wants me, is gonna come correct
With no hesitation
And the utmost respect

silk.

I really don't know how to deal with death
I don't want my tears to keep you here
But I fear for your departure
Are you okay?
Did you make it to the other side?
Who took your hand and made the transition all
right?

You are forever in our hearts
Your name is written in the sand
Nobody will ever replace you
Nobody can

Waterfall

I want to feel the mist in my face
To be surrounded by trees

I arrive
Unstrap my pack
Unlace my shoes
Dip in the pool
Rest my eyes

My vision is clear
I feel at peace here

purification

silk.

Death gets so much harder as I get older
It hurts to know
People only leave their memories once they're gone
Nothing worth having lasts forever
It makes me think of my parents and their buried
treasures
What haven't they told me? What haven't I asked?
I get my mouth from my mom
No wonder I have so much sass
I have to think before I speak because death doesn't
give notifications
Death doesn't come with an ETA or turn by turn
instructions
      Instead it rips people from your arms
         and pries their hearts from your palms
      It's not fair
         just like everything in this life
         it's not fair at all
We have to teach ourselves how to live through it
Let the tears come as they please
I am grateful
for everything
The good, the bad
Every. Single. Memory.

2020
Can you loosen your grip?

There has been so much loss
Lives, homes, sanity
So much pain
Even more anxiety
These issues are black holes
Consume, consume, consume
There's no escape
but we see the light
Luckily, my generation is informed, educated
and ready to fight

silk.

What's wrong? Oh, so many things. Do you have the time to listen to me overthink?

Everyday I feel like the world is on fire. No justice, no peace. Covid-19. Racist police. Lord, we are tired. I don't want to complain; I am so grateful. But I carry this weight in my chest. Instead of a heart, it feels like an anchor.

I've been having bad dreams. I wake up in pools of sweat from my own screams; loud bangs & violence. I can't find peace in my own silence. I thought I was happy. But my hurt is deep. It's like I have a gaping wound, but no one can see me bleed. I hide it well, so I think anyway.

Don't get me wrong… I am happy. I am grateful. I am just used to sitting in sadness & fatigue. My tears & heart wrenches have kept me company. And my life is so good. Who am I to be ungrateful? I don't know how to fix this. I don't know how to fix me. But, I think I'm able.

Forgive my moment of weakness.
The mirage will be back tomorrow.

God, please keep us safe
In your grace
I don't consider myself religious
But I still Thank You
at the end of each day.

silk.

Thank you for your time
For allowing me to enter your heart
To invade your thoughts
I'll leave you with a positive note

"Keep your head up." - Tupac

Made in USA - Kendallville, IN
1205511_9798559250823
12.04.2020 0728